A TRUE BOOK™

The Seven Continents
Antarctica

KAREN KELLAHER

Children's Press
An Imprint of Scholas

D1377166

Content Consultant

Beatrix Schlarb-Ridley, Ph.D.

Director of Innovations and Impact

British Antarctic Survey

Library of Congress Cataloging-in-Publication Data

Names: Kellaher, Karen, author.

Title: Antarctica / by Karen Kellaher.

Description: New York, NY : Children's Press, an imprint of Scholastic Inc., 2019. | Series: A true book |
   Includes bibliographical references and index.

Identifiers: LCCN 2018027252| ISBN 9780531128053 (library binding : alk. paper) | ISBN 9780531134139
   (pbk. : alk. paper)

Subjects: LCSH: Antarctica—Discovery and exploration. | CYAC: Antarctica—Juvenile literature.

Classification: LCC G860 .K45 2019 | DDC 919.89—dc23

LC record available at https://lccn.loc.gov/2018027252

All rights reserved. Published in 2019 by Children's Press, an imprint of Scholastic Inc.

Printed in North Mankato, MN, USA 113

SCHOLASTIC, CHILDREN'S PRESS, A TRUE BOOK™, and associated logos are trademarks and/or
registered trademarks of Scholastic Inc.

Scholastic Inc., 557 Broadway, New York, NY 10012

2 3 4 5 6 7 8 9 10 R 28 27 26 25 24 23 22 21 20

Front: Antarctica

Back: Tourists photographing a penguin

Find the Truth!

Everything you are about to read is true *except* for one of the sentences on this page.

Which one is **TRUE**?

T or F Antarctica is considered a desert.

T or F Polar bears are a common sight in Antarctica.

Find the answers in this book.

Contents

THE BIG TRUTH!

Too Many Tourists?

Emperor penguins

4

Airplane landing in Antarctica

Tourist ship

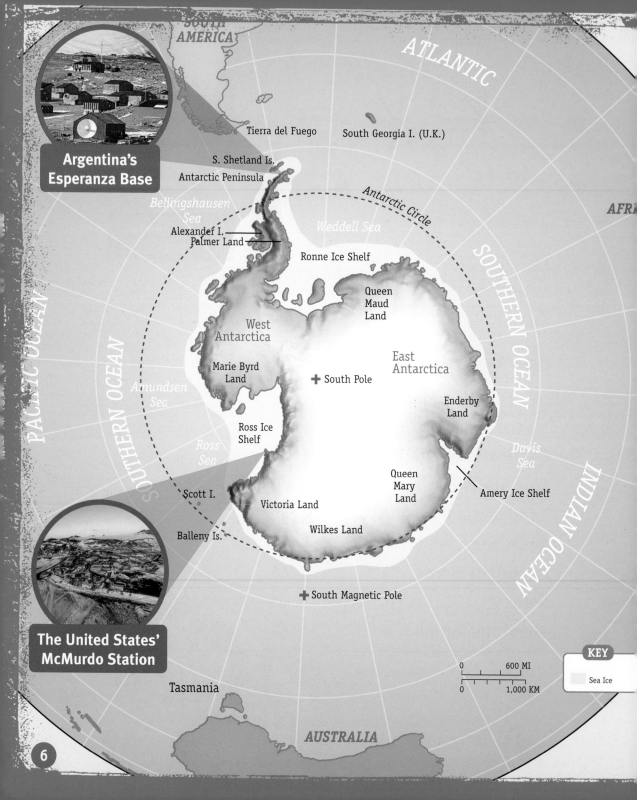

SOUTH AMERICA

ATLANTIC

Tierra del Fuego

South Georgia I. (U.K.)

Argentina's Esperanza Base

S. Shetland Is.

Antarctic Peninsula

Bellingshausen Sea

AFR

Antarctic Circle

Weddell Sea

SOUTHERN OCEAN

Alexander I.
Palmer Land

Ronne Ice Shelf

Queen Maud Land

West Antarctica

East Antarctica

PACIFIC OCEAN

Marie Byrd Land

+ South Pole

SOUTHERN OCEAN

Amundsen Sea

Enderby Land

Ross Ice Shelf

Davis Sea

Ross Sea

Queen Mary Land

Amery Ice Shelf

INDIAN OCEAN

Scott I.

Victoria Land

Balleny Is.

Wilkes Land

The United States' McMurdo Station

+ South Magnetic Pole

Tasmania

KEY

Sea Ice

0			600 MI
0			1,000 KM

AUSTRALIA

Continent Close-up

Antarctica is Earth's most extreme continent. It sits at the bottom of the world and includes the South Pole, Earth's southernmost point. It is colder and windier than any other place on Earth. Antarctica is almost completely covered in a thick sheet of ice and is surrounded by frosty ocean waters. No humans live in Antarctica permanently, and there are no countries or cities there. But people from around the world visit the continent to do scientific research.

Land area	5.4 million square miles (14 million square kilometers)
Average thickness of ice sheet	1.3 miles (2.16 kilometers)
Number of countries	0
Number of permanent research stations	About 75
Year-round population	About 1,000
Population during the Antarctic summer (around November to March)	About 4,000
Fast fact	People did not set foot in Antarctica until the 1800s.

Layers of ice often form on the surface of the ocean surrounding Antarctica.

CHAPTER 1

Land and Climate

Hundreds of millions of years ago, Antarctica was at the center of a giant landmass called Gondwana. Much of Gondwana was lush green forest. But about 180 million years ago, Gondwana began to break apart. This process formed several of today's continents. When the breakup was over, Antarctica was alone at the bottom of Earth. About 34 million years ago, Antarctica experienced a deep freeze. Its green forests were no more. Today, most of the continent is covered in an ice sheet that is as big as the United States and Mexico combined!

East and West

Antarctica has three main regions. East Antarctica is the largest. It is an icy **plateau**. West Antarctica is made up mostly of mountainous islands that are held together by ice. These

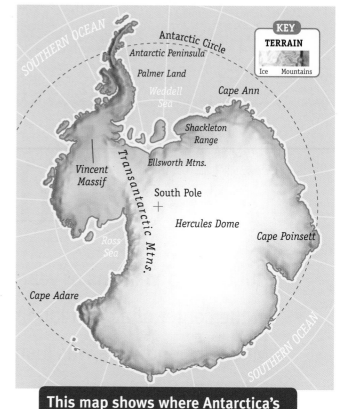

This map shows where Antarctica's flat ice and mountainous areas are.

two regions are divided by the Transantarctic Mountains, which run up and down the continent. The third region is the Antarctic **Peninsula**, a small section in the far west that sticks out into the ocean like an arm. Antarctica also includes many small islands that surround the mainland.

Water All Around

For hundreds of years, the water surrounding Antarctica was considered part of the Atlantic, Indian, and Pacific oceans. But by 2000, many scientists agreed that this area should be its own ocean. They began calling it the Southern Ocean. Some of the ocean areas that are closest to the Antarctic coast are known as seas. Two of the largest are the Ross Sea and the Weddell Sea. In addition, Antarctica has rivers and lakes beneath its ice. Scientists are still learning about these hidden waterways.

As Antarctic ice slowly melts, it can form arches and other interesting shapes.

Types of Ice

The ice that covers most of Antarctica is called an ice sheet or an ice cap. It is made of freshwater. Along the edges of the continent, giant slabs of this ice extend out over the ocean. These are called ice shelves. Sometimes parts break off and fall into the ocean, creating **icebergs**. This process is called calving. It can sound like an explosion! Another kind of ice in Antarctica is sea ice. It is frozen ocean water. It grows every year during the Antarctic winter. Much of it melts during the summer.

Icebergs come in all shapes and sizes. Some are gigantic.

The word *iceberg* comes from Dutch words meaning "ice mountain."

Steam escaping from underground caves in Antarctica is instantly frozen, forming ice towers.

Feel the Chill

Antarctica is the coldest place on Earth. Even in summer, the average temperature at the South Pole is −18 degrees Fahrenheit (−28 degrees Celsius).

Because of the way Earth is tilted as it orbits the sun, Antarctica has only two seasons—summer and winter. During its summer, Antarctica faces the sun. This means it is light 24 hours a day at the height of summer. During Antarctic winter, the continent is tilted away from the sun. That means almost six months of darkness and even colder temperatures.

Strong Antarctic winds often whip up the snow that is already on the ground.

Icy Desert

The Antarctic ice sheet contains a whopping 70 percent of the world's freshwater. But believe it or not, it rarely snows or rains in central Antarctica. In fact, the middle of the continent gets less than 2 inches (5 centimeters) of **precipitation** a year! That means Antarctica is officially a desert. So where does all of its ice come from? Because Antarctica is so cold, the little snow that does fall on its surface rarely melts. Instead, it has built up over millions of years.

Blood Falls

This waterfall in East Antarctica gets its creepy name from its bright-red water. The water flows from cracks in a **glacier**. For decades, scientists thought its color came from tiny red living things called algae. But in 2017, researchers made a big discovery. They learned that the water flows from a lake and rivers buried beneath the glacier. The lake and rivers are rich in iron. The iron-rich water turns red when it hits the air— just like a bicycle gets rusty when it's left outside!

This waterfall is in no hurry. Scientists think it takes water about 1.5 million years to make its way through the glacier. The water is super salty, which keeps it from freezing.

Each year, Antarctica's emperor penguins march inland from the edges of Antarctica to begin their breeding season.

CHAPTER 2

Plants and Animals

It is not easy to live in Antarctica. Only a few tiny plants and insects make their homes in the continent's icy inner areas. But things are livelier along the coast. There, fish and other sea creatures fill the water. Seabirds soar in the skies. Penguins and seals often come ashore to raise their young. One animal you won't see anywhere in Antarctica is a polar bear. Polar bears live only in the Arctic region, at the opposite end of the globe.

Plenty of Penguins

When it comes to Antarctica's wildlife, penguins rule. Four species of these seabirds live along the coast of mainland Antarctica. Several others live on the Antarctic islands. The biggest of them is the emperor penguin. It stands almost 4 feet (1.2 meters) tall and can weigh more than 80 pounds (36 kilograms)! Penguins are built to handle Antarctica's frigid air and water. They have a thick layer of fat to keep them warm and a set of waxy, waterproof feathers that keep their skin dry. These birds can't fly, but they are excellent swimmers.

The Weddell seal is named for British explorer and hunter James Weddell.

Home Sweet Home

When they aren't in the water, penguins live on shore in groups called rookeries. This is where female penguins lay their eggs. After an egg hatches, penguin parents take turns caring for their new chick. One parent stays with the chick while the other hunts for food.

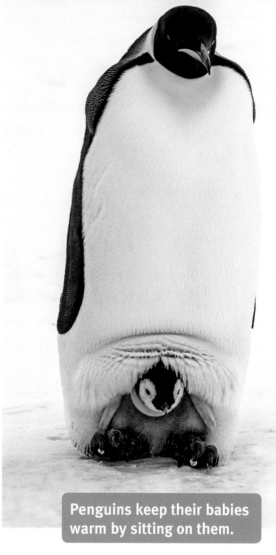

Penguins keep their babies warm by sitting on them.

The hunter plunges into the ocean to dine on fish, squid, and tiny creatures called krill. Penguin parents bring food back for the chick until the chick is old enough to hunt on its own.

Antarctic terns have black heads in summer, but grow white streaks during winter.

In the Skies

Even though penguins do not fly, the skies above Antarctica are hardly empty. Many flying seabirds, including albatrosses, terns, petrels, and skuas, call the continent home. Every summer, millions of these birds breed along the coasts of Antarctica and its islands. They feast on fish and other creatures in the ocean waters. When the Antarctic winter arrives, many of these waters freeze. The seabirds then **migrate** north in search of food. But they return again the following year. Some of them travel thousands of miles each year.

Under the Waves

The seas around Antarctica are home to seals, whales, fish, squid, and many other creatures. One of the smallest animals is the shrimplike krill. It is less than 2 inches (5 cm) long. The largest creature in Antarctica's waters—and in the world—is the blue whale. It can grow to be 100 feet (30.5 m) long and weigh 150 tons (136 metric tons). This hungry marine **mammal** can gulp down as many as 40 million krill a day. That's almost 4 tons (3.6 metric tons) of food!

Krill are an important food for many Antarctic animals.

Where Are the Trees?

Not a single tree or bush grows in Antarctica. The few spots on the continent that are not covered in ice are too rocky and windy for most plants to live. So what does grow? Antarctica has about 100 species of moss. Mosses are flat, flowerless plants that grow like carpets on rocks. Two species of small flowering plants survive in certain areas. These plants, Antarctic hair grass and Antarctic pearlwort, are found on the Antarctic Peninsula and nearby islands. The continent also has simple plantlike life called lichens and algae.

Mosses add bright color to a landscape where grasses, trees, and other plants cannot grow.

Species in Trouble

Some of Antarctica's plant and animal species are in danger of dying out, mainly due to human activities. Here are just a few:

Antarctic Blue Whale

Home: Summers in the Southern Ocean around Antarctica

This endangered subspecies was once hunted in large numbers for its meat and blubber, which was used to make oil. Today blue whales are sometimes hit by boats and tangled in fishing gear.

Sooty Albatross

Home: Southern Ocean and southern parts of other oceans

Several kinds of albatross, including this species, are in danger. They accidentally eat plastic trash in the ocean. They also get caught in fishing lines.

Fin Whale

Home: Southern Ocean, though very rare (found more often in other oceans)

These whales were hunted widely in the 1900s. Like the blue whale, this endangered species is now threatened by ship traffic and fishing gear.

Antarctic and Patagonian Toothfish

Home: Southern Ocean

Not all fishing crews in Antarctica follow the rules. Some people worry that toothfish and certain other species are being overfished. These species are not endangered yet, but scientists are keeping a close eye on them.

Too Many Tourists?

Tens of thousands of tourists visit Antarctica each year. Some sail along the coastline in ships or fly over the continent in small planes. Others come ashore to see the icy scenery up close. Some people worry that this tourism will ruin Antarctica's unspoiled environment. They want to stop it. But others disagree.

This chart explores both sides of the debate. What do you think?

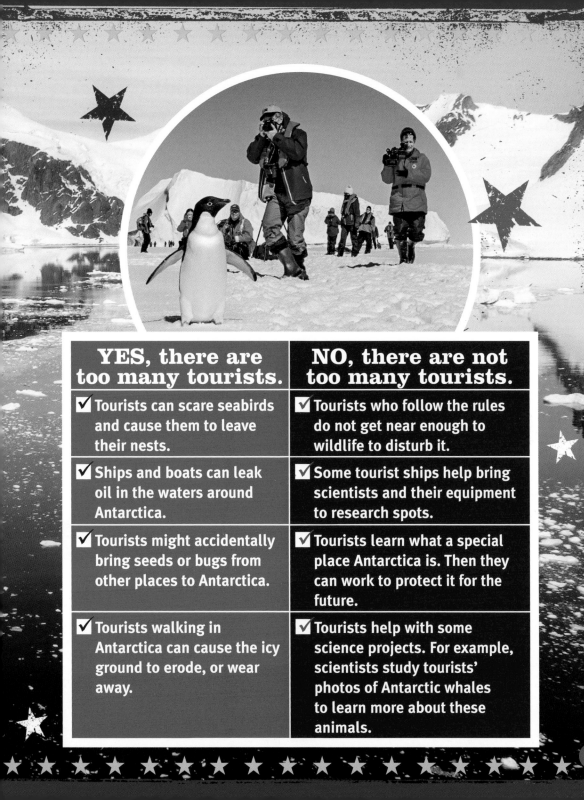

YES, there are too many tourists.	NO, there are not too many tourists.
☑ Tourists can scare seabirds and cause them to leave their nests.	☑ Tourists who follow the rules do not get near enough to wildlife to disturb it.
☑ Ships and boats can leak oil in the waters around Antarctica.	☑ Some tourist ships help bring scientists and their equipment to research spots.
☑ Tourists might accidentally bring seeds or bugs from other places to Antarctica.	☑ Tourists learn what a special place Antarctica is. Then they can work to protect it for the future.
☑ Tourists walking in Antarctica can cause the icy ground to erode, or wear away.	☑ Tourists help with some science projects. For example, scientists study tourists' photos of Antarctic whales to learn more about these animals.

The D'Urville Sea, located off the coast of Antarctica, is named for Jules Dumont d'Urville.

French explorer Jules Dumont d'Urville led an expedition to explore the Antarctic region in the late 1830s.

CHAPTER 3

A Peek at the Past

People guessed that Antarctica existed long before they ever saw it. More than 2,000 years ago, the ancient Greeks knew about the Arctic, the area of ice and land around the North Pole. They named it *Arktos*, or "the bear," after a **constellation** of stars in the northern night sky. A Greek philosopher named Aristotle thought that there must be a similar region at the bottom of the planet as well. He named this land *Antarktikos*, or "opposite to the bear."

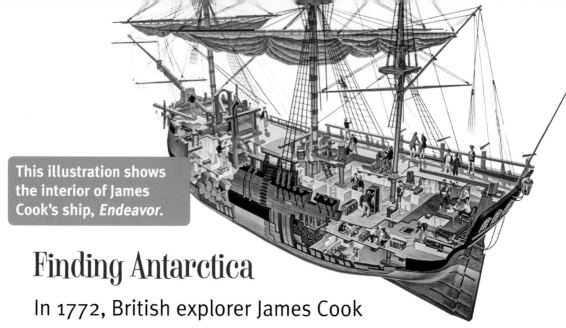

Finding Antarctica

In 1772, British explorer James Cook set out to find Antarctica. He spent three years at sea, but he never saw it. Cook did spot plenty of seals, though. He told people back home. Soon, seal hunters from all over the world were heading for the Southern Ocean. Over the years, they sailed farther and farther south. Finally, in 1820, several crews glimpsed Antarctica. The next year, American hunter John Davis is believed to have landed briefly on the Antarctic Peninsula. Many historians think Davis and his crew were the first people to set foot on the continent.

The Age of Exploration Begins

As the seal population decreased, people paid less attention to Antarctica. But by the late 1800s and early 1900s, interest grew again. Crews began hunting whales in Antarctic waters. And many countries began sending explorers and scientists to the continent. These **expeditions** mapped much of the continent's coast and explored parts of the interior. Some even braved the long, cold Antarctic winters. This period of exploration beginning in about 1900 is known as the Heroic Age of Antarctic Exploration.

A crew of whalers stands atop a blue whale that was caught in Antarctic waters in the 1930s.

Race to the South Pole

The South Pole is the southernmost point on Earth. It lies in Antarctica, hundreds of miles from any coast. In 1901, an expedition led by Britain's Robert Falcon Scott set out for the pole. However, illness and a shortage of food forced the team to turn back. A few years later, another team got within about 100 miles (161 km) of the pole. They too ran out of supplies and had to give up.

Antarctica's Timeline

350 BCE
Aristotle writes of a land called *Antarktikos*.

1821
Seal hunter John Davis and his crew are thought to be the first to set foot on the continent.

350 BCE	1820 CE	1821	1911

1820 CE
Crews from Russia, Britain, and the United States are the first to see Antarctica.

1911
A crew led by Norway's Roald Amundsen reaches the South Pole.

30

In 1911, the race to the pole heated up. Two teams—one led by Norwegian Roald Amundsen and another led again by Scott—were determined to get to the pole. Amundsen's team got there first, on December 14, 1911. Scott's team, which started out 11 days after Amundsen's and stopped to do research, arrived a month later. They found a Norwegian flag already planted at the pole. Sadly, Scott and his entire team died on their return trip.

1921–1922
British explorer Ernest Shackleton leads his third and final expedition to Antarctica, marking the end of a period known as the Heroic Age of Antarctic Exploration.

1961
The Antarctic Treaty, signed in 1959, takes effect.

1921–1922 > **1929** > **1961** > **Today**

1929
Richard Byrd of the United States makes the first airplane flight over the South Pole.

Today
Thousands of researchers work in dozens of stations around Antarctica.

The flags of the first countries to sign the Antarctic Treaty fly in Antarctica.

A Continent for Everyone

Over time, several countries tried to claim parts of Antarctica as their own. But soon people came up with a plan for sharing the continent. In 1957 and 1958, scientists from 12 countries ran research stations in Antarctica as part of a worldwide science event called the International Geophysical Year. In 1959, those nations wrote and signed the Antarctic **Treaty**. This agreement said that no country could claim Antarctica and that the continent could only be used for peaceful research and exploration. Today, more than 50 countries have agreed to the treaty.

Finding the South Pole

Roald Amundsen wrote this account of reaching the South Pole:

On the morning of December 14, the weather was fine, just as if it had been made for arriving at the Pole. ... At three in the afternoon the sled drivers all yelled "Halt!" Their tools showed that we had reached the Pole. We proceeded to the greatest and most solemn act of the whole journey—the planting of our flag. ... Five weather-beaten, frost-bitten fists grasped the pole, raised the waving flag in the air, and planted it as the first at the geographical South Pole.

Amundsen and his team had arrived on the edge of Antarctica in January 1911, about a year earlier.

Explorers often put flags in the ground to claim land for their home countries.

THINK ABOUT IT: Why do you think it took so long to reach the South Pole?

Amundsen used sled dogs to help him reach the South Pole.

The passage has been adapted and shortened by Scholastic for young readers. Source: The South Pole by Roald Amundsen.

The U.S.-run McMurdo Station has been operating since December 1955.

CHAPTER 4

Antarctica Today

No one lives in Antarctica permanently. But every Antarctic summer, about 4,000 scientists and support staff stay on the continent to conduct research. As many as 1,000 of these men and women also brave the intense Antarctic winter. In addition, more than 30,000 tourists visit Antarctica during the summer months. About a quarter of the tourists come from the United States. Tourists travel with trained guides. Most come ashore only for brief periods.

At Home on the Ice

About 30 countries operate more than 70 research stations in Antarctica. Argentina, Chile, Russia, and China have the most stations. Some of the facilities are small and are only open during Antarctica's summer months. But about 40 of them are used all year long. The largest station is McMurdo, run by the United States. It has about 100 buildings, and about 1,000 people work there during the summer. It is like a small town.

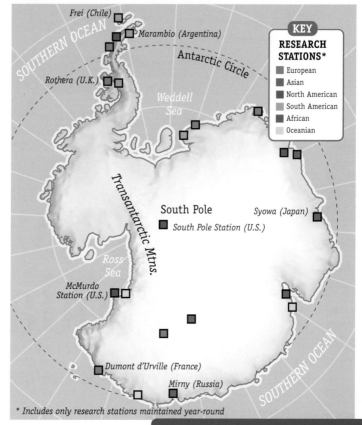

KEY

RESEARCH STATIONS*

- European
- Asian
- North American
- South American
- African
- Oceanian

Frei (Chile)

Marambio (Argentina)

SOUTHERN OCEAN

Antarctic Circle

Rothera (U.K.)

Weddell Sea

Transantarctic Mtns.

South Pole
South Pole Station (U.S.)

Syowa (Japan)

Ross Sea

McMurdo Station (U.S.)

Dumont d'Urville (France)

Mirny (Russia)

SOUTHERN OCEAN

* Includes only research stations maintained year-round

This map shows the locations of some of Antarctica's major research stations.

Stocking Up

Antarctica has no factories and few natural **resources**. Everything people need must be delivered by boat or plane. Deliveries can be made only in the summer. In winter, Antarctica's waters become too icy for boats to get through. The constant darkness also makes flying dangerous. Research teams face another challenge, too—what to do with their trash. Today, they ship almost all of it back to their home countries. But sometimes equipment and old buildings have been left behind on the ice.

Special airplanes are equipped with skis to help them land on Antarctica's icy surface.

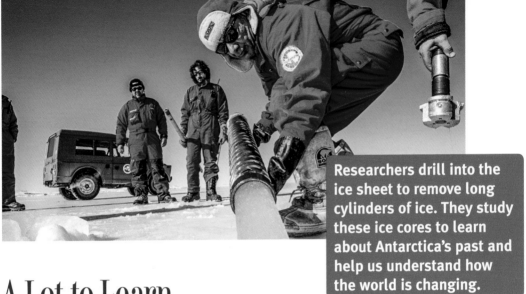

Researchers drill into the ice sheet to remove long cylinders of ice. They study these ice cores to learn about Antarctica's past and help us understand how the world is changing.

A Lot to Learn

Scientists in Antarctica study the land, ice, air, seas, wildlife, and more. Recently, a big focus of their research has been how climate change might be affecting Antarctica and the rest of the globe. For more than 100 years, Earth's average temperature has been rising slowly. Most scientists say that a main cause is the burning of fossil fuels. In Antarctica, researchers have observed that some of the ice on the Antarctic Peninsula is melting, contributing to a rise in sea levels. They think Earth's warm-up may be to blame.

Cool Science

Here's a look at some of the projects scientists have been working on in Antarctica.

Seals on Duty

What's a good way to measure the temperature of Antarctica's seas? Researchers are putting sensors on the foreheads of elephant seals and Weddell seals!

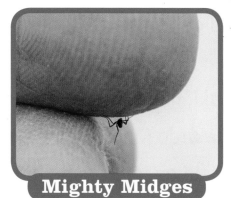

Mighty Midges

These insects, less than 0.25 inch (6.4 millimeters) long, are the largest land animals to spend their whole lives in Antarctica's interior. Scientists are studying them to learn how they survive the extreme cold.

Penguin Clues

Examining old penguin eggshells and feathers helps scientists learn how penguins and their diets have changed over time.

Space Rocks

Scientists collect meteorites, pieces of rock or metal that have fallen to Earth's surface from outer space. Meteorites are easy to spot on Antarctica's icy surface. Crews study them to learn more about the solar system.

Chilling Out

Many research stations have libraries, gyms, and game rooms where people can relax during their time off. And many scientists head outdoors to ski, hike, and play sports. Some run in the McMurdo Marathon, a 26.2-mile (42 km) race that is held on the ice shelf every January. A few even take part in polar plunges. They cut holes in the ice and jump into the water below—then quickly run back inside to get warm!

A runner passes a curious penguin during a marathon.

The Antarctic ice sheet is 3 miles (4.8 km) thick in some spots.

Antarctica's Future

The Antarctic Treaty still governs what people can do in Antarctica. Representatives of many of the treaty's signees meet once a year. They discuss issues facing the continent and sometimes make new rules. For example, in 1991, new environmental rules were passed. One says that no country can mine for oil, gas, or minerals in Antarctica until at least the year 2048. Through rules like this one, officials hope to protect the icy continent for many years to come. ★

Destination

CEREMONIAL SOUTH POLE

The flags of the first countries that signed the Antarctic Treaty surround this fancy marker. It's where most visitors take photos. But because the marker is on a slowly moving ice sheet, the real South Pole is a few hundred feet away!

MT. EREBUS

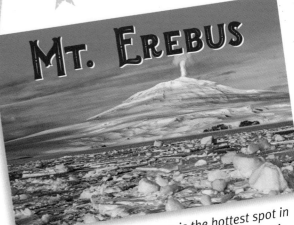

The inside of this volcano is the hottest spot in Antarctica. It has a pool of melted rock that's about 1,700°F (927°C)! Erebus has frequent small eruptions. It spews gases into the air and spits out chunks of rock.

McMURDO DRY VALLEYS

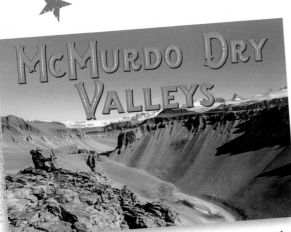

These valleys are among the only spots in Antarctica not covered in ice. One reason is that super strong winds blow away any moisture. Scientists think the dry valleys are a lot like the surface of Mars.

DECEPTION ISLAND

This horseshoe-shaped island is part of an Antarctic volcano. Heat from deep inside Earth creates warm springs that people can sit in.

Antarctica

MOUNT VINSON

At a height of 16,050 feet (4,892 m), the peak of this mountain is the highest point in Antarctica.

PEGASUS WRECK

In 1970, a plane carrying 80 scientists crashed into the Antarctic surface. All of the passengers survived, but the wreckage still sits on the ice.

BORCHGREVINK'S HUTS

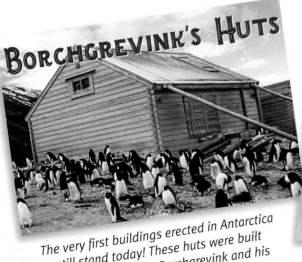

The very first buildings erected in Antarctica still stand today! These huts were built by explorer Carsten Borchgrevink and his crew in 1899. They were the first people to spend a winter in Antarctica.

LAKE VOSTOK

cored 2.2 miles

Antarctica is thought to have many lakes hidden beneath its ice. Vostok is the largest. Scientists believe the water contains tiny, single-celled living things.

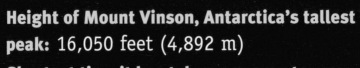

True Statistics: Continental Extremes

Height of Mount Vinson, Antarctica's tallest peak: 16,050 feet (4,892 m)

Shortest time it has taken a person to cross Antarctica on skis: 57 days

Percentage of the world's freshwater that is found in Antarctica: 70

Size of the largest iceberg ever to break off of Antarctica: 183 mi. (294 km) long and 23 mi. (37 km) wide

Speed of the super strong winds that sometimes blow from Antarctica's middle toward the sea: 200 mi. (322 km) per hour

Amount that global sea levels would rise if all of Antarctica's ice melted: About 180 feet (55 m)

Did you find the truth?

(T) Antarctica is considered a desert.

(F) Polar bears are a common sight in Antarctica.

Resources

Books

Hanel, Rachael. *Can You Survive Antarctica? An Interactive Survival Adventure*. Mankato, MN: Capstone, 2011.

Mara, Wil. *Antarctica*. New York: Children's Press, 2017.

Osborne, Mary Pope, and Natalie Pope Boyce. *Penguins and Antarctica: A Nonfiction Companion to Magic Tree House Merlin Mission #12*. New York: Random House, 2008.

Squire, Ann O. *Penguins*. New York: Children's Press, 2007.

Taylor, Barbara. *Arctic and Antarctic*. London: DK Eyewitness, 2012.

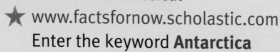

Visit this Scholastic website for more information on Antarctica:
★ www.factsfornow.scholastic.com
Enter the keyword **Antarctica**

Important Words

constellation (kon-stuh-LAY-shuhn) a group of stars that form a shape or pattern

expeditions (ek-spuh-DISH-uhnz) long journeys for a special purpose

glacier (GLAY-shur) a huge sheet of ice found in mountain valleys or polar regions

icebergs (ISE-bergz) large masses of ice that have broken off from a glacier and are floating in the sea

mammal (MAM-uhl) a warm-blooded animal with a backbone; female mammals produce milk to feed their young

migrate (MYE-grate) to move from one place to another, especially according to the seasons

peninsula (puh-NIN-suh-luh) a piece of land that sticks out from a larger landmass and is almost completely surrounded by water

plateau (plah-TOH) an area of level ground that is higher than the surrounding area

precipitation (prih-sip-ih-TAY-shuhn) rain, hail, sleet, or snow

resources (REE-sore-sez) things that are valuable or useful to a place or a person

treaty (TREE-tee) a formal agreement between two or more countries

Index

Page numbers in **bold** indicate illustrations.

About the Author

Karen Kellaher is an editor in Scholastic's classroom magazine division and has written more than 20 books for kids and teachers. She holds a bachelor's degree in communications from the University of Scranton (Pennsylvania) and a master's degree combining elementary education and publishing from New York University's Gallatin School of Individualized Study.